Caring for someone with Dementia is often a stressful, ever-changing experience.

Dementia symptoms and issues are often seen as random, and uncontrollable. However, having up to date, accurate information about your patient or loved one can often lead to the identification of patterns and triggers, that help to ease to caring process. With this information, you will be better equipped to deal with these behaviours and health problems.

This notekeeping journal has been developed for the care of Dementia and Alzhiemers patients, with notes for all the key aspects of this horrible disease. It is designed to track the daily and weekly needs and patterns, and help to establish the most efficient and effective care process.

With the daily logs, you track things like mood, medication and treatment, positives and negatives, toileting and feeding, and all other key information needed for a caregiver. Then, with the weekly recap, you are asked to summarise and more importantly look for patterns that will ultimately assist you in giving the best care you can. These patterns may come in the form of triggers, moods at different times of day and what causes them, and what has been working.

By spending a few minutes each day analysing these aspects, you will eventually be able to save time and stress by only doing what is working, and avoiding what is not. It is important to note that Dementia patients will change over time, some more rapidly than others, but by keeping a journal or logbook, these patterns will be able to be swiftly noticed, and caring routines will be able to be adapted to these changing needs.

USING THIS BOOK

Track moods at different times of day. Use notes to identify triggers / reasons if possible

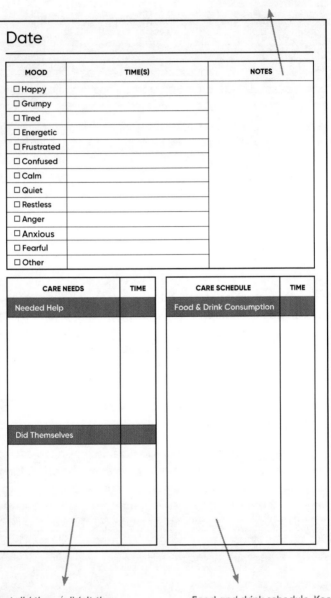

Date

MOOD	TIME(S)	NOTES
☐ Happy		
☐ Grumpy		
☐ Tired		
☐ Energetic		
☐ Frustrated		
☐ Confused		
☐ Calm		
☐ Quiet		
☐ Restless		
☐ Anger		
☐ Anxious		
☐ Fearful		
☐ Other		

CARE NEEDS	TIME
Needed Help	
Did Themselves	

CARE SCHEDULE	TIME
Food & Drink Consumption	

What did they / didn't they need help with (E.g. bathroom, feeding). This will change over time

Food and drink schedule. Keep notes of ease / attitudes

Bathroom Schedule.

Keep notes of medication effects or side effects. Also keep notes or questions for next Doctor visit

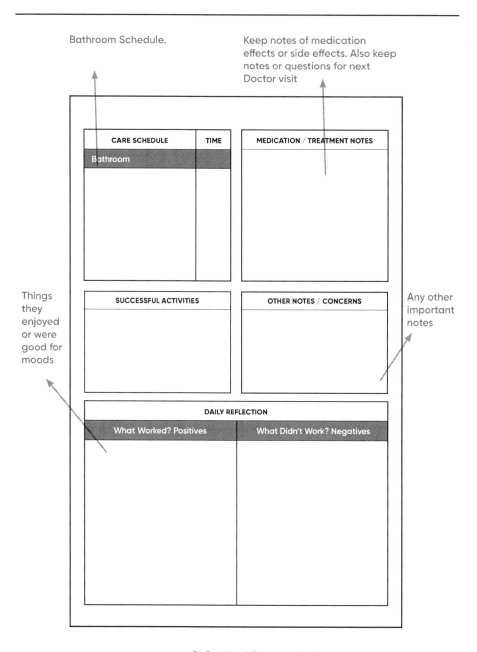

CARE SCHEDULE	TIME
Bathroom	

MEDICATION / TREATMENT NOTES

Things they enjoyed or were good for moods

SUCCESSFUL ACTIVITIES

OTHER NOTES / CONCERNS

Any other important notes

DAILY REFLECTION	
What Worked? Positives	What Didn't Work? Negatives

Reflection / Summary for the day. This is where you reflect on what worked and what didn't, and look for patterns that will assist you in improving your care routine.

Date

MOOD	TIME(S)	NOTES
☐ Happy		
☐ Grumpy		
☐ Tired		
☐ Energetic		
☐ Frustrated		
☐ Confused		
☐ Calm		
☐ Quiet		
☐ Restless		
☐ Anger		
☐ Anxious		
☐ Fearful		
☐ Other		

CARE NEEDS	TIME
Needed Help	
Did Themselves	

CARE SCHEDULE	TIME
Food & Drink Consumption	

CARE SCHEDULE	TIME
Bathroom	

MEDICATION / TREATMENT NOTES

SUCCESSFUL ACTIVITIES

OTHER NOTES / CONCERNS

DAILY REFLECTION	
What Worked? Positives	What Didn't Work? Negatives

Date

MOOD	TIME(S)	NOTES
☐ Happy		
☐ Grumpy		
☐ Tired		
☐ Energetic		
☐ Frustrated		
☐ Confused		
☐ Calm		
☐ Quiet		
☐ Restless		
☐ Anger		
☐ Anxious		
☐ Fearful		
☐ Other		

CARE NEEDS	TIME
Needed Help	
Did Themselves	

CARE SCHEDULE	TIME
Food & Drink Consumption	

CARE SCHEDULE	TIME
Bathroom	

MEDICATION / TREATMENT NOTES

SUCCESSFUL ACTIVITIES

OTHER NOTES / CONCERNS

DAILY REFLECTION	
What Worked? Positives	What Didn't Work? Negatives

Date

MOOD	TIME(S)	NOTES
☐ Happy		
☐ Grumpy		
☐ Tired		
☐ Energetic		
☐ Frustrated		
☐ Confused		
☐ Calm		
☐ Quiet		
☐ Restless		
☐ Anger		
☐ Anxious		
☐ Fearful		
☐ Other		

CARE NEEDS	TIME
Needed Help	
Did Themselves	

CARE SCHEDULE	TIME
Food & Drink Consumption	

CARE SCHEDULE	TIME
Bathroom	

MEDICATION / TREATMENT NOTES

SUCCESSFUL ACTIVITIES

OTHER NOTES / CONCERNS

DAILY REFLECTION	
What Worked? Positives	What Didn't Work? Negatives

Date

MOOD	TIME(S)	NOTES
☐ Happy		
☐ Grumpy		
☐ Tired		
☐ Energetic		
☐ Frustrated		
☐ Confused		
☐ Calm		
☐ Quiet		
☐ Restless		
☐ Anger		
☐ Anxious		
☐ Fearful		
☐ Other		

CARE NEEDS	TIME
Needed Help	
Did Themselves	

CARE SCHEDULE	TIME
Food & Drink Consumption	

CARE SCHEDULE	TIME
Bathroom	

MEDICATION / TREATMENT NOTES

SUCCESSFUL ACTIVITIES

OTHER NOTES / CONCERNS

DAILY REFLECTION

What Worked? Positives	What Didn't Work? Negatives

Date

MOOD	TIME(S)	NOTES
☐ Happy		
☐ Grumpy		
☐ Tired		
☐ Energetic		
☐ Frustrated		
☐ Confused		
☐ Calm		
☐ Quiet		
☐ Restless		
☐ Anger		
☐ Anxious		
☐ Fearful		
☐ Other		

CARE NEEDS	TIME
Needed Help	
Did Themselves	

CARE SCHEDULE	TIME
Food & Drink Consumption	

CARE SCHEDULE	TIME
Bathroom	

MEDICATION / TREATMENT NOTES

SUCCESSFUL ACTIVITIES

OTHER NOTES / CONCERNS

DAILY REFLECTION	
What Worked? Positives	What Didn't Work? Negatives

Date

MOOD	TIME(S)	NOTES
☐ Happy		
☐ Grumpy		
☐ Tired		
☐ Energetic		
☐ Frustrated		
☐ Confused		
☐ Calm		
☐ Quiet		
☐ Restless		
☐ Anger		
☐ Anxious		
☐ Fearful		
☐ Other		

CARE NEEDS	TIME
Needed Help	
Did Themselves	

CARE SCHEDULE	TIME
Food & Drink Consumption	

CARE SCHEDULE	TIME
Bathroom	

MEDICATION / TREATMENT NOTES

SUCCESSFUL ACTIVITIES

OTHER NOTES / CONCERNS

DAILY REFLECTION

What Worked? Positives	What Didn't Work? Negatives

Date

MOOD	TIME(S)	NOTES
☐ Happy		
☐ Grumpy		
☐ Tired		
☐ Energetic		
☐ Frustrated		
☐ Confused		
☐ Calm		
☐ Quiet		
☐ Restless		
☐ Anger		
☐ Anxious		
☐ Fearful		
☐ Other		

CARE NEEDS	TIME
Needed Help	
Did Themselves	

CARE SCHEDULE	TIME
Food & Drink Consumption	

CARE SCHEDULE	TIME
Bathroom	

MEDICATION / TREATMENT NOTES

SUCCESSFUL ACTIVITIES

OTHER NOTES / CONCERNS

DAILY REFLECTION	
What Worked? Positives	What Didn't Work? Negatives

Weekly Recap & Patterns

MAIN MOOD(S) / TIMES / PATTERNS

CARE NEEDS PATTERNS

Needed Help

Did Themselves

CARE SCHEDULE PATTERNS

Food & Drink Consumption

CARE SCHEDULE PATTERNS	MEDICATION / TREATMENT NOTES
Bathroom	

SUCCESSFUL WEEKLY ACTIVITIES	OTHER NOTES / WEEKLY CONCERNS

WEEKLY REFLECTION

What Worked? Positives	What Didn't Work? Negatives

USING THIS BOOK

Track moods at different times of day. Use notes to identify triggers / reasons if possible

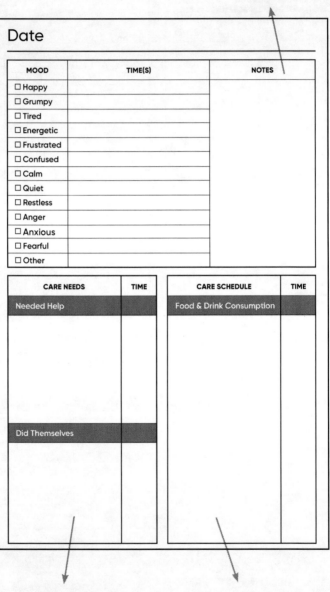

Date

MOOD	TIME(S)	NOTES
☐ Happy		
☐ Grumpy		
☐ Tired		
☐ Energetic		
☐ Frustrated		
☐ Confused		
☐ Calm		
☐ Quiet		
☐ Restless		
☐ Anger		
☐ Anxious		
☐ Fearful		
☐ Other		

CARE NEEDS	TIME
Needed Help	
Did Themselves	

CARE SCHEDULE	TIME
Food & Drink Consumption	

What did they / didn't they need help with (E.g. bathroom, feeding). This will change over time

Food and drink schedule. Keep notes of ease / attitudes

Bathroom Schedule.

Keep notes of medication effects or side effects. Also keep notes or questions for next Doctor visit

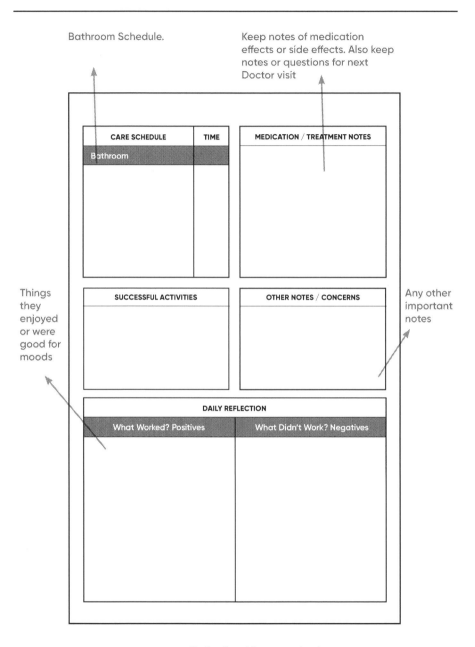

CARE SCHEDULE	TIME
Bathroom	

MEDICATION / TREATMENT NOTES

SUCCESSFUL ACTIVITIES

OTHER NOTES / CONCERNS

DAILY REFLECTION	
What Worked? Positives	What Didn't Work? Negatives

Things they enjoyed or were good for moods

Any other important notes

Reflection / Summary for the day. This is where you reflect on what worked and what didn't, and look for patterns that will assist you in improving your care routine.

Date

MOOD	TIME(S)	NOTES
☐ Happy		
☐ Grumpy		
☐ Tired		
☐ Energetic		
☐ Frustrated		
☐ Confused		
☐ Calm		
☐ Quiet		
☐ Restless		
☐ Anger		
☐ Anxious		
☐ Fearful		
☐ Other		

CARE NEEDS	TIME
Needed Help	
Did Themselves	

CARE SCHEDULE	TIME
Food & Drink Consumption	

CARE SCHEDULE	TIME
Bathroom	

MEDICATION / TREATMENT NOTES

SUCCESSFUL ACTIVITIES

OTHER NOTES / CONCERNS

DAILY REFLECTION

What Worked? Positives	What Didn't Work? Negatives

Date

MOOD	TIME(S)	NOTES
☐ Happy		
☐ Grumpy		
☐ Tired		
☐ Energetic		
☐ Frustrated		
☐ Confused		
☐ Calm		
☐ Quiet		
☐ Restless		
☐ Anger		
☐ Anxious		
☐ Fearful		
☐ Other		

CARE NEEDS	TIME
Needed Help	
Did Themselves	

CARE SCHEDULE	TIME
Food & Drink Consumption	

CARE SCHEDULE	TIME
Bathroom	

MEDICATION / TREATMENT NOTES

SUCCESSFUL ACTIVITIES

OTHER NOTES / CONCERNS

DAILY REFLECTION	
What Worked? Positives	What Didn't Work? Negatives

Date

MOOD	TIME(S)	NOTES
☐ Happy		
☐ Grumpy		
☐ Tired		
☐ Energetic		
☐ Frustrated		
☐ Confused		
☐ Calm		
☐ Quiet		
☐ Restless		
☐ Anger		
☐ Anxious		
☐ Fearful		
☐ Other		

CARE NEEDS	TIME
Needed Help	
Did Themselves	

CARE SCHEDULE	TIME
Food & Drink Consumption	

CARE SCHEDULE	TIME	MEDICATION / TREATMENT NOTES
Bathroom		

SUCCESSFUL ACTIVITIES	OTHER NOTES / CONCERNS

DAILY REFLECTION	
What Worked? Positives	What Didn't Work? Negatives

Date

MOOD	TIME(S)	NOTES
☐ Happy		
☐ Grumpy		
☐ Tired		
☐ Energetic		
☐ Frustrated		
☐ Confused		
☐ Calm		
☐ Quiet		
☐ Restless		
☐ Anger		
☐ Anxious		
☐ Fearful		
☐ Other		

CARE NEEDS	TIME
Needed Help	
Did Themselves	

CARE SCHEDULE	TIME
Food & Drink Consumption	

CARE SCHEDULE	TIME
Bathroom	

MEDICATION / TREATMENT NOTES

SUCCESSFUL ACTIVITIES

OTHER NOTES / CONCERNS

DAILY REFLECTION	
What Worked? Positives	What Didn't Work? Negatives

Date

MOOD	TIME(S)	NOTES
☐ Happy		
☐ Grumpy		
☐ Tired		
☐ Energetic		
☐ Frustrated		
☐ Confused		
☐ Calm		
☐ Quiet		
☐ Restless		
☐ Anger		
☐ Anxious		
☐ Fearful		
☐ Other		

CARE NEEDS	TIME
Needed Help	
Did Themselves	

CARE SCHEDULE	TIME
Food & Drink Consumption	

CARE SCHEDULE	TIME
Bathroom	

MEDICATION / TREATMENT NOTES

SUCCESSFUL ACTIVITIES

OTHER NOTES / CONCERNS

DAILY REFLECTION	
What Worked? Positives	What Didn't Work? Negatives

Date

MOOD	TIME(S)	NOTES
☐ Happy		
☐ Grumpy		
☐ Tired		
☐ Energetic		
☐ Frustrated		
☐ Confused		
☐ Calm		
☐ Quiet		
☐ Restless		
☐ Anger		
☐ Anxious		
☐ Fearful		
☐ Other		

CARE NEEDS	TIME
Needed Help	
Did Themselves	

CARE SCHEDULE	TIME
Food & Drink Consumption	

CARE SCHEDULE	TIME	MEDICATION / TREATMENT NOTES
Bathroom		

SUCCESSFUL ACTIVITIES	OTHER NOTES / CONCERNS

DAILY REFLECTION	
What Worked? Positives	What Didn't Work? Negatives

Date

MOOD	TIME(S)	NOTES
☐ Happy		
☐ Grumpy		
☐ Tired		
☐ Energetic		
☐ Frustrated		
☐ Confused		
☐ Calm		
☐ Quiet		
☐ Restless		
☐ Anger		
☐ Anxious		
☐ Fearful		
☐ Other		

CARE NEEDS	TIME
Needed Help	
Did Themselves	

CARE SCHEDULE	TIME
Food & Drink Consumption	

CARE SCHEDULE	TIME
Bathroom	

MEDICATION / TREATMENT NOTES

SUCCESSFUL ACTIVITIES

OTHER NOTES / CONCERNS

DAILY REFLECTION	
What Worked? Positives	What Didn't Work? Negatives

Weekly Recap & Patterns

MAIN MOOD(S) / TIMES / PATTERNS

CARE NEEDS PATTERNS	CARE SCHEDULE PATTERNS
Needed Help	**Food & Drink Consumption**
Did Themselves	

CARE SCHEDULE PATTERNS	MEDICATION / TREATMENT NOTES
Bathroom	

SUCCESSFUL WEEKLY ACTIVITIES	OTHER NOTES / WEEKLY CONCERNS

WEEKLY REFLECTION	
What Worked? Positives	What Didn't Work? Negatives

Date

MOOD	TIME(S)	NOTES
☐ Happy		
☐ Grumpy		
☐ Tired		
☐ Energetic		
☐ Frustrated		
☐ Confused		
☐ Calm		
☐ Quiet		
☐ Restless		
☐ Anger		
☐ Anxious		
☐ Fearful		
☐ Other		

CARE NEEDS	TIME
Needed Help	
Did Themselves	

CARE SCHEDULE	TIME
Food & Drink Consumption	

CARE SCHEDULE	TIME
Bathroom	

MEDICATION / TREATMENT NOTES

SUCCESSFUL ACTIVITIES

OTHER NOTES / CONCERNS

DAILY REFLECTION	
What Worked? Positives	What Didn't Work? Negatives

Date

MOOD	TIME(S)	NOTES
☐ Happy		
☐ Grumpy		
☐ Tired		
☐ Energetic		
☐ Frustrated		
☐ Confused		
☐ Calm		
☐ Quiet		
☐ Restless		
☐ Anger		
☐ Anxious		
☐ Fearful		
☐ Other		

CARE NEEDS	TIME
Needed Help	
Did Themselves	

CARE SCHEDULE	TIME
Food & Drink Consumption	

CARE SCHEDULE	TIME
Bathroom	

MEDICATION / TREATMENT NOTES

SUCCESSFUL ACTIVITIES

OTHER NOTES / CONCERNS

DAILY REFLECTION	
What Worked? Positives	What Didn't Work? Negatives

Date

MOOD	TIME(S)	NOTES
☐ Happy		
☐ Grumpy		
☐ Tired		
☐ Energetic		
☐ Frustrated		
☐ Confused		
☐ Calm		
☐ Quiet		
☐ Restless		
☐ Anger		
☐ Anxious		
☐ Fearful		
☐ Other		

CARE NEEDS	TIME
Needed Help	
Did Themselves	

CARE SCHEDULE	TIME
Food & Drink Consumption	

CARE SCHEDULE	TIME
Bathroom	

MEDICATION / TREATMENT NOTES

SUCCESSFUL ACTIVITIES

OTHER NOTES / CONCERNS

DAILY REFLECTION	
What Worked? Positives	What Didn't Work? Negatives

Date

MOOD	TIME(S)	NOTES
☐ Happy		
☐ Grumpy		
☐ Tired		
☐ Energetic		
☐ Frustrated		
☐ Confused		
☐ Calm		
☐ Quiet		
☐ Restless		
☐ Anger		
☐ Anxious		
☐ Fearful		
☐ Other		

CARE NEEDS	TIME
Needed Help	
Did Themselves	

CARE SCHEDULE	TIME
Food & Drink Consumption	

CARE SCHEDULE	TIME
Bathroom	

MEDICATION / TREATMENT NOTES

SUCCESSFUL ACTIVITIES

OTHER NOTES / CONCERNS

DAILY REFLECTION

What Worked? Positives	What Didn't Work? Negatives

Date

MOOD	TIME(S)	NOTES
☐ Happy		
☐ Grumpy		
☐ Tired		
☐ Energetic		
☐ Frustrated		
☐ Confused		
☐ Calm		
☐ Quiet		
☐ Restless		
☐ Anger		
☐ Anxious		
☐ Fearful		
☐ Other		

CARE NEEDS	TIME
Needed Help	
Did Themselves	

CARE SCHEDULE	TIME
Food & Drink Consumption	

CARE SCHEDULE	TIME
Bathroom	

MEDICATION / TREATMENT NOTES

SUCCESSFUL ACTIVITIES

OTHER NOTES / CONCERNS

DAILY REFLECTION	
What Worked? Positives	What Didn't Work? Negatives

Date

MOOD	TIME(S)	NOTES
☐ Happy		
☐ Grumpy		
☐ Tired		
☐ Energetic		
☐ Frustrated		
☐ Confused		
☐ Calm		
☐ Quiet		
☐ Restless		
☐ Anger		
☐ Anxious		
☐ Fearful		
☐ Other		

CARE NEEDS	TIME
Needed Help	
Did Themselves	

CARE SCHEDULE	TIME
Food & Drink Consumption	

CARE SCHEDULE	TIME
Bathroom	

MEDICATION / TREATMENT NOTES

SUCCESSFUL ACTIVITIES

OTHER NOTES / CONCERNS

DAILY REFLECTION	
What Worked? Positives	What Didn't Work? Negatives

Date

MOOD	TIME(S)	NOTES
☐ Happy		
☐ Grumpy		
☐ Tired		
☐ Energetic		
☐ Frustrated		
☐ Confused		
☐ Calm		
☐ Quiet		
☐ Restless		
☐ Anger		
☐ Anxious		
☐ Fearful		
☐ Other		

CARE NEEDS	TIME
Needed Help	
Did Themselves	

CARE SCHEDULE	TIME
Food & Drink Consumption	

CARE SCHEDULE	TIME
Bathroom	

MEDICATION / TREATMENT NOTES

SUCCESSFUL ACTIVITIES

OTHER NOTES / CONCERNS

DAILY REFLECTION	
What Worked? Positives	What Didn't Work? Negatives

Weekly Recap & Patterns

MAIN MOOD(S) / TIMES / PATTERNS

CARE NEEDS PATTERNS

Needed Help

Did Themselves

CARE SCHEDULE PATTERNS

Food & Drink Consumption

CARE SCHEDULE PATTERNS	MEDICATION / TREATMENT NOTES
Bathroom	

SUCCESSFUL WEEKLY ACTIVITIES	OTHER NOTES / WEEKLY CONCERNS

WEEKLY REFLECTION

What Worked? Positives	What Didn't Work? Negatives

Date

MOOD	TIME(S)	NOTES
☐ Happy		
☐ Grumpy		
☐ Tired		
☐ Energetic		
☐ Frustrated		
☐ Confused		
☐ Calm		
☐ Quiet		
☐ Restless		
☐ Anger		
☐ Anxious		
☐ Fearful		
☐ Other		

CARE NEEDS	TIME
Needed Help	
Did Themselves	

CARE SCHEDULE	TIME
Food & Drink Consumption	

CARE SCHEDULE	TIME	MEDICATION / TREATMENT NOTES
Bathroom		

SUCCESSFUL ACTIVITIES	OTHER NOTES / CONCERNS

DAILY REFLECTION	
What Worked? Positives	What Didn't Work? Negatives

Date

MOOD	TIME(S)	NOTES
☐ Happy		
☐ Grumpy		
☐ Tired		
☐ Energetic		
☐ Frustrated		
☐ Confused		
☐ Calm		
☐ Quiet		
☐ Restless		
☐ Anger		
☐ Anxious		
☐ Fearful		
☐ Other		

CARE NEEDS	TIME
Needed Help	
Did Themselves	

CARE SCHEDULE	TIME
Food & Drink Consumption	

CARE SCHEDULE	TIME
Bathroom	

MEDICATION / TREATMENT NOTES

SUCCESSFUL ACTIVITIES

OTHER NOTES / CONCERNS

DAILY REFLECTION	
What Worked? Positives	What Didn't Work? Negatives

Date

MOOD	TIME(S)	NOTES
☐ Happy		
☐ Grumpy		
☐ Tired		
☐ Energetic		
☐ Frustrated		
☐ Confused		
☐ Calm		
☐ Quiet		
☐ Restless		
☐ Anger		
☐ Anxious		
☐ Fearful		
☐ Other		

CARE NEEDS	TIME
Needed Help	
Did Themselves	

CARE SCHEDULE	TIME
Food & Drink Consumption	

CARE SCHEDULE	TIME
Bathroom	

MEDICATION / TREATMENT NOTES

SUCCESSFUL ACTIVITIES

OTHER NOTES / CONCERNS

DAILY REFLECTION	
What Worked? Positives	What Didn't Work? Negatives

Date

MOOD	TIME(S)	NOTES
☐ Happy		
☐ Grumpy		
☐ Tired		
☐ Energetic		
☐ Frustrated		
☐ Confused		
☐ Calm		
☐ Quiet		
☐ Restless		
☐ Anger		
☐ Anxious		
☐ Fearful		
☐ Other		

CARE NEEDS	TIME
Needed Help	
Did Themselves	

CARE SCHEDULE	TIME
Food & Drink Consumption	

CARE SCHEDULE	TIME	MEDICATION / TREATMENT NOTES
Bathroom		

SUCCESSFUL ACTIVITIES	OTHER NOTES / CONCERNS

DAILY REFLECTION	
What Worked? Positives	What Didn't Work? Negatives

Date

MOOD	TIME(S)	NOTES
☐ Happy		
☐ Grumpy		
☐ Tired		
☐ Energetic		
☐ Frustrated		
☐ Confused		
☐ Calm		
☐ Quiet		
☐ Restless		
☐ Anger		
☐ Anxious		
☐ Fearful		
☐ Other		

CARE NEEDS	TIME
Needed Help	
Did Themselves	

CARE SCHEDULE	TIME
Food & Drink Consumption	

CARE SCHEDULE	TIME
Bathroom	

MEDICATION / TREATMENT NOTES

SUCCESSFUL ACTIVITIES

OTHER NOTES / CONCERNS

DAILY REFLECTION	
What Worked? Positives	What Didn't Work? Negatives

Date

MOOD	TIME(S)	NOTES
☐ Happy		
☐ Grumpy		
☐ Tired		
☐ Energetic		
☐ Frustrated		
☐ Confused		
☐ Calm		
☐ Quiet		
☐ Restless		
☐ Anger		
☐ Anxious		
☐ Fearful		
☐ Other		

CARE NEEDS	TIME
Needed Help	
Did Themselves	

CARE SCHEDULE	TIME
Food & Drink Consumption	

CARE SCHEDULE	TIME
Bathroom	

MEDICATION / TREATMENT NOTES

SUCCESSFUL ACTIVITIES

OTHER NOTES / CONCERNS

DAILY REFLECTION	
What Worked? Positives	What Didn't Work? Negatives

Date

MOOD	TIME(S)	NOTES
☐ Happy		
☐ Grumpy		
☐ Tired		
☐ Energetic		
☐ Frustrated		
☐ Confused		
☐ Calm		
☐ Quiet		
☐ Restless		
☐ Anger		
☐ Anxious		
☐ Fearful		
☐ Other		

CARE NEEDS	TIME
Needed Help	
Did Themselves	

CARE SCHEDULE	TIME
Food & Drink Consumption	

CARE SCHEDULE	TIME
Bathroom	

MEDICATION / TREATMENT NOTES

SUCCESSFUL ACTIVITIES

OTHER NOTES / CONCERNS

DAILY REFLECTION	
What Worked? Positives	What Didn't Work? Negatives

Weekly Recap & Patterns

MAIN MOOD(S) / TIMES / PATTERNS

CARE NEEDS PATTERNS	CARE SCHEDULE PATTERNS
Needed Help	Food & Drink Consumption
Did Themselves	

CARE SCHEDULE PATTERNS	MEDICATION / TREATMENT NOTES
Bathroom	

SUCCESSFUL WEEKLY ACTIVITIES	OTHER NOTES / WEEKLY CONCERNS

WEEKLY REFLECTION	
What Worked? Positives	What Didn't Work? Negatives

Date

MOOD	TIME(S)	NOTES
☐ Happy		
☐ Grumpy		
☐ Tired		
☐ Energetic		
☐ Frustrated		
☐ Confused		
☐ Calm		
☐ Quiet		
☐ Restless		
☐ Anger		
☐ Anxious		
☐ Fearful		
☐ Other		

CARE NEEDS	TIME
Needed Help	
Did Themselves	

CARE SCHEDULE	TIME
Food & Drink Consumption	

CARE SCHEDULE	TIME
Bathroom	

MEDICATION / TREATMENT NOTES

SUCCESSFUL ACTIVITIES

OTHER NOTES / CONCERNS

DAILY REFLECTION

What Worked? Positives	What Didn't Work? Negatives

Date

MOOD	TIME(S)	NOTES
☐ Happy		
☐ Grumpy		
☐ Tired		
☐ Energetic		
☐ Frustrated		
☐ Confused		
☐ Calm		
☐ Quiet		
☐ Restless		
☐ Anger		
☐ Anxious		
☐ Fearful		
☐ Other		

CARE NEEDS	TIME
Needed Help	
Did Themselves	

CARE SCHEDULE	TIME
Food & Drink Consumption	

CARE SCHEDULE	TIME
Bathroom	

MEDICATION / TREATMENT NOTES

SUCCESSFUL ACTIVITIES

OTHER NOTES / CONCERNS

DAILY REFLECTION	
What Worked? Positives	What Didn't Work? Negatives

Date

MOOD	TIME(S)	NOTES
☐ Happy		
☐ Grumpy		
☐ Tired		
☐ Energetic		
☐ Frustrated		
☐ Confused		
☐ Calm		
☐ Quiet		
☐ Restless		
☐ Anger		
☐ Anxious		
☐ Fearful		
☐ Other		

CARE NEEDS	TIME
Needed Help	
Did Themselves	

CARE SCHEDULE	TIME
Food & Drink Consumption	

CARE SCHEDULE	TIME
Bathroom	

MEDICATION / TREATMENT NOTES

SUCCESSFUL ACTIVITIES

OTHER NOTES / CONCERNS

DAILY REFLECTION	
What Worked? Positives	What Didn't Work? Negatives

Date

MOOD	TIME(S)	NOTES
☐ Happy		
☐ Grumpy		
☐ Tired		
☐ Energetic		
☐ Frustrated		
☐ Confused		
☐ Calm		
☐ Quiet		
☐ Restless		
☐ Anger		
☐ Anxious		
☐ Fearful		
☐ Other		

CARE NEEDS	TIME
Needed Help	
Did Themselves	

CARE SCHEDULE	TIME
Food & Drink Consumption	

CARE SCHEDULE	TIME
Bathroom	

MEDICATION / TREATMENT NOTES

SUCCESSFUL ACTIVITIES

OTHER NOTES / CONCERNS

DAILY REFLECTION	
What Worked? Positives	What Didn't Work? Negatives

Date

MOOD	TIME(S)	NOTES
☐ Happy		
☐ Grumpy		
☐ Tired		
☐ Energetic		
☐ Frustrated		
☐ Confused		
☐ Calm		
☐ Quiet		
☐ Restless		
☐ Anger		
☐ Anxious		
☐ Fearful		
☐ Other		

CARE NEEDS	TIME
Needed Help	
Did Themselves	

CARE SCHEDULE	TIME
Food & Drink Consumption	

CARE SCHEDULE	TIME
Bathroom	

MEDICATION / TREATMENT NOTES

SUCCESSFUL ACTIVITIES

OTHER NOTES / CONCERNS

DAILY REFLECTION	
What Worked? Positives	What Didn't Work? Negatives

Date

MOOD	TIME(S)	NOTES
☐ Happy		
☐ Grumpy		
☐ Tired		
☐ Energetic		
☐ Frustrated		
☐ Confused		
☐ Calm		
☐ Quiet		
☐ Restless		
☐ Anger		
☐ Anxious		
☐ Fearful		
☐ Other		

CARE NEEDS	TIME
Needed Help	
Did Themselves	

CARE SCHEDULE	TIME
Food & Drink Consumption	

CARE SCHEDULE	TIME
Bathroom	

MEDICATION / TREATMENT NOTES

SUCCESSFUL ACTIVITIES

OTHER NOTES / CONCERNS

DAILY REFLECTION

What Worked? Positives	What Didn't Work? Negatives

Date

MOOD	TIME(S)	NOTES
☐ Happy		
☐ Grumpy		
☐ Tired		
☐ Energetic		
☐ Frustrated		
☐ Confused		
☐ Calm		
☐ Quiet		
☐ Restless		
☐ Anger		
☐ Anxious		
☐ Fearful		
☐ Other		

CARE NEEDS	TIME
Needed Help	
Did Themselves	

CARE SCHEDULE	TIME
Food & Drink Consumption	

CARE SCHEDULE	TIME
Bathroom	

MEDICATION / TREATMENT NOTES

SUCCESSFUL ACTIVITIES

OTHER NOTES / CONCERNS

DAILY REFLECTION

What Worked? Positives	What Didn't Work? Negatives

Weekly Recap & Patterns

MAIN MOOD(S) / TIMES / PATTERNS

CARE NEEDS PATTERNS

Needed Help

Did Themselves

CARE SCHEDULE PATTERNS

Food & Drink Consumption

CARE SCHEDULE PATTERNS

Bathroom

MEDICATION / TREATMENT NOTES

SUCCESSFUL WEEKLY ACTIVITIES

OTHER NOTES / WEEKLY CONCERNS

WEEKLY REFLECTION

What Worked? Positives	What Didn't Work? Negatives

Date

MOOD	TIME(S)	NOTES
☐ Happy		
☐ Grumpy		
☐ Tired		
☐ Energetic		
☐ Frustrated		
☐ Confused		
☐ Calm		
☐ Quiet		
☐ Restless		
☐ Anger		
☐ Anxious		
☐ Fearful		
☐ Other		

CARE NEEDS	TIME
Needed Help	
Did Themselves	

CARE SCHEDULE	TIME
Food & Drink Consumption	

CARE SCHEDULE	TIME
Bathroom	

MEDICATION / TREATMENT NOTES

SUCCESSFUL ACTIVITIES

OTHER NOTES / CONCERNS

DAILY REFLECTION

What Worked? Positives	What Didn't Work? Negatives

Date

MOOD	TIME(S)	NOTES
☐ Happy		
☐ Grumpy		
☐ Tired		
☐ Energetic		
☐ Frustrated		
☐ Confused		
☐ Calm		
☐ Quiet		
☐ Restless		
☐ Anger		
☐ Anxious		
☐ Fearful		
☐ Other		

CARE NEEDS	TIME
Needed Help	
Did Themselves	

CARE SCHEDULE	TIME
Food & Drink Consumption	

CARE SCHEDULE	TIME
Bathroom	

MEDICATION / TREATMENT NOTES

SUCCESSFUL ACTIVITIES

OTHER NOTES / CONCERNS

DAILY REFLECTION

What Worked? Positives	What Didn't Work? Negatives

Date

MOOD	TIME(S)	NOTES
☐ Happy		
☐ Grumpy		
☐ Tired		
☐ Energetic		
☐ Frustrated		
☐ Confused		
☐ Calm		
☐ Quiet		
☐ Restless		
☐ Anger		
☐ Anxious		
☐ Fearful		
☐ Other		

CARE NEEDS	TIME
Needed Help	
Did Themselves	

CARE SCHEDULE	TIME
Food & Drink Consumption	

CARE SCHEDULE	TIME
Bathroom	

MEDICATION / TREATMENT NOTES

SUCCESSFUL ACTIVITIES

OTHER NOTES / CONCERNS

DAILY REFLECTION

What Worked? Positives	What Didn't Work? Negatives

Date

MOOD	TIME(S)	NOTES
☐ Happy		
☐ Grumpy		
☐ Tired		
☐ Energetic		
☐ Frustrated		
☐ Confused		
☐ Calm		
☐ Quiet		
☐ Restless		
☐ Anger		
☐ Anxious		
☐ Fearful		
☐ Other		

CARE NEEDS	TIME
Needed Help	
Did Themselves	

CARE SCHEDULE	TIME
Food & Drink Consumption	

CARE SCHEDULE	TIME
Bathroom	

MEDICATION / TREATMENT NOTES

SUCCESSFUL ACTIVITIES

OTHER NOTES / CONCERNS

DAILY REFLECTION

What Worked? Positives	What Didn't Work? Negatives

Date

MOOD	TIME(S)	NOTES
☐ Happy		
☐ Grumpy		
☐ Tired		
☐ Energetic		
☐ Frustrated		
☐ Confused		
☐ Calm		
☐ Quiet		
☐ Restless		
☐ Anger		
☐ Anxious		
☐ Fearful		
☐ Other		

CARE NEEDS	TIME
Needed Help	
Did Themselves	

CARE SCHEDULE	TIME
Food & Drink Consumption	

CARE SCHEDULE	TIME
Bathroom	

MEDICATION / TREATMENT NOTES

SUCCESSFUL ACTIVITIES

OTHER NOTES / CONCERNS

DAILY REFLECTION

What Worked? Positives	What Didn't Work? Negatives

Date

MOOD	TIME(S)	NOTES
☐ Happy		
☐ Grumpy		
☐ Tired		
☐ Energetic		
☐ Frustrated		
☐ Confused		
☐ Calm		
☐ Quiet		
☐ Restless		
☐ Anger		
☐ Anxious		
☐ Fearful		
☐ Other		

CARE NEEDS	TIME
Needed Help	
Did Themselves	

CARE SCHEDULE	TIME
Food & Drink Consumption	

CARE SCHEDULE	TIME
Bathroom	

MEDICATION / TREATMENT NOTES

SUCCESSFUL ACTIVITIES

OTHER NOTES / CONCERNS

DAILY REFLECTION

What Worked? Positives	What Didn't Work? Negatives

Date

MOOD	TIME(S)	NOTES
☐ Happy		
☐ Grumpy		
☐ Tired		
☐ Energetic		
☐ Frustrated		
☐ Confused		
☐ Calm		
☐ Quiet		
☐ Restless		
☐ Anger		
☐ Anxious		
☐ Fearful		
☐ Other		

CARE NEEDS	TIME
Needed Help	
Did Themselves	

CARE SCHEDULE	TIME
Food & Drink Consumption	

CARE SCHEDULE	TIME
Bathroom	

MEDICATION / TREATMENT NOTES

SUCCESSFUL ACTIVITIES

OTHER NOTES / CONCERNS

DAILY REFLECTION

What Worked? Positives	What Didn't Work? Negatives

Weekly Recap & Patterns

MAIN MOOD(S) / TIMES / PATTERNS

CARE NEEDS PATTERNS

Needed Help

Did Themselves

CARE SCHEDULE PATTERNS

Food & Drink Consumption

CARE SCHEDULE PATTERNS

Bathroom

MEDICATION / TREATMENT NOTES

SUCCESSFUL WEEKLY ACTIVITIES

OTHER NOTES / WEEKLY CONCERNS

WEEKLY REFLECTION

What Worked? Positives	What Didn't Work? Negatives

Date

MOOD	TIME(S)	NOTES
☐ Happy		
☐ Grumpy		
☐ Tired		
☐ Energetic		
☐ Frustrated		
☐ Confused		
☐ Calm		
☐ Quiet		
☐ Restless		
☐ Anger		
☐ Anxious		
☐ Fearful		
☐ Other		

CARE NEEDS	TIME
Needed Help	
Did Themselves	

CARE SCHEDULE	TIME
Food & Drink Consumption	

CARE SCHEDULE	TIME
Bathroom	

MEDICATION / TREATMENT NOTES

SUCCESSFUL ACTIVITIES

OTHER NOTES / CONCERNS

DAILY REFLECTION

What Worked? Positives	What Didn't Work? Negatives

Date

MOOD	TIME(S)	NOTES
☐ Happy		
☐ Grumpy		
☐ Tired		
☐ Energetic		
☐ Frustrated		
☐ Confused		
☐ Calm		
☐ Quiet		
☐ Restless		
☐ Anger		
☐ Anxious		
☐ Fearful		
☐ Other		

CARE NEEDS	TIME
Needed Help	
Did Themselves	

CARE SCHEDULE	TIME
Food & Drink Consumption	

CARE SCHEDULE	TIME
Bathroom	

MEDICATION / TREATMENT NOTES

SUCCESSFUL ACTIVITIES

OTHER NOTES / CONCERNS

DAILY REFLECTION

What Worked? Positives	What Didn't Work? Negatives

Date

MOOD	TIME(S)	NOTES
☐ Happy		
☐ Grumpy		
☐ Tired		
☐ Energetic		
☐ Frustrated		
☐ Confused		
☐ Calm		
☐ Quiet		
☐ Restless		
☐ Anger		
☐ Anxious		
☐ Fearful		
☐ Other		

CARE NEEDS	TIME
Needed Help	
Did Themselves	

CARE SCHEDULE	TIME
Food & Drink Consumption	

CARE SCHEDULE	TIME
Bathroom	

MEDICATION / TREATMENT NOTES

SUCCESSFUL ACTIVITIES

OTHER NOTES / CONCERNS

DAILY REFLECTION	
What Worked? Positives	What Didn't Work? Negatives

Date

MOOD	TIME(S)	NOTES
☐ Happy		
☐ Grumpy		
☐ Tired		
☐ Energetic		
☐ Frustrated		
☐ Confused		
☐ Calm		
☐ Quiet		
☐ Restless		
☐ Anger		
☐ Anxious		
☐ Fearful		
☐ Other		

CARE NEEDS	TIME
Needed Help	
Did Themselves	

CARE SCHEDULE	TIME
Food & Drink Consumption	

CARE SCHEDULE	TIME
Bathroom	

MEDICATION / TREATMENT NOTES

SUCCESSFUL ACTIVITIES

OTHER NOTES / CONCERNS

DAILY REFLECTION	
What Worked? Positives	What Didn't Work? Negatives

Date

MOOD	TIME(S)	NOTES
☐ Happy		
☐ Grumpy		
☐ Tired		
☐ Energetic		
☐ Frustrated		
☐ Confused		
☐ Calm		
☐ Quiet		
☐ Restless		
☐ Anger		
☐ Anxious		
☐ Fearful		
☐ Other		

CARE NEEDS	TIME
Needed Help	
Did Themselves	

CARE SCHEDULE	TIME
Food & Drink Consumption	

CARE SCHEDULE	TIME
Bathroom	

MEDICATION / TREATMENT NOTES

SUCCESSFUL ACTIVITIES

OTHER NOTES / CONCERNS

DAILY REFLECTION

What Worked? Positives	What Didn't Work? Negatives

Date

MOOD	TIME(S)	NOTES
☐ Happy		
☐ Grumpy		
☐ Tired		
☐ Energetic		
☐ Frustrated		
☐ Confused		
☐ Calm		
☐ Quiet		
☐ Restless		
☐ Anger		
☐ Anxious		
☐ Fearful		
☐ Other		

CARE NEEDS	TIME
Needed Help	
Did Themselves	

CARE SCHEDULE	TIME
Food & Drink Consumption	

CARE SCHEDULE	TIME
Bathroom	

MEDICATION / TREATMENT NOTES

SUCCESSFUL ACTIVITIES

OTHER NOTES / CONCERNS

DAILY REFLECTION

What Worked? Positives	What Didn't Work? Negatives

Date

MOOD	TIME(S)	NOTES
☐ Happy		
☐ Grumpy		
☐ Tired		
☐ Energetic		
☐ Frustrated		
☐ Confused		
☐ Calm		
☐ Quiet		
☐ Restless		
☐ Anger		
☐ Anxious		
☐ Fearful		
☐ Other		

CARE NEEDS	TIME
Needed Help	
Did Themselves	

CARE SCHEDULE	TIME
Food & Drink Consumption	

CARE SCHEDULE	TIME
Bathroom	

MEDICATION / TREATMENT NOTES

SUCCESSFUL ACTIVITIES

OTHER NOTES / CONCERNS

DAILY REFLECTION

What Worked? Positives	What Didn't Work? Negatives

Weekly Recap & Patterns

MAIN MOOD(S) / TIMES / PATTERNS

CARE NEEDS PATTERNS

Needed Help

Did Themselves

CARE SCHEDULE PATTERNS

Food & Drink Consumption

CARE SCHEDULE PATTERNS	MEDICATION / TREATMENT NOTES
Bathroom	

SUCCESSFUL WEEKLY ACTIVITIES	OTHER NOTES / WEEKLY CONCERNS

WEEKLY REFLECTION

What Worked? Positives	What Didn't Work? Negatives

Date

MOOD	TIME(S)	NOTES
☐ Happy		
☐ Grumpy		
☐ Tired		
☐ Energetic		
☐ Frustrated		
☐ Confused		
☐ Calm		
☐ Quiet		
☐ Restless		
☐ Anger		
☐ Anxious		
☐ Fearful		
☐ Other		

CARE NEEDS	TIME
Needed Help	
Did Themselves	

CARE SCHEDULE	TIME
Food & Drink Consumption	

CARE SCHEDULE	TIME
Bathroom	

MEDICATION / TREATMENT NOTES

SUCCESSFUL ACTIVITIES

OTHER NOTES / CONCERNS

DAILY REFLECTION

What Worked? Positives	What Didn't Work? Negatives

Date

MOOD	TIME(S)	NOTES
☐ Happy		
☐ Grumpy		
☐ Tired		
☐ Energetic		
☐ Frustrated		
☐ Confused		
☐ Calm		
☐ Quiet		
☐ Restless		
☐ Anger		
☐ Anxious		
☐ Fearful		
☐ Other		

CARE NEEDS	TIME
Needed Help	
Did Themselves	

CARE SCHEDULE	TIME
Food & Drink Consumption	

CARE SCHEDULE	TIME
Bathroom	

MEDICATION / TREATMENT NOTES

SUCCESSFUL ACTIVITIES

OTHER NOTES / CONCERNS

DAILY REFLECTION

What Worked? Positives	What Didn't Work? Negatives

Date

MOOD	TIME(S)	NOTES
☐ Happy		
☐ Grumpy		
☐ Tired		
☐ Energetic		
☐ Frustrated		
☐ Confused		
☐ Calm		
☐ Quiet		
☐ Restless		
☐ Anger		
☐ Anxious		
☐ Fearful		
☐ Other		

CARE NEEDS	TIME
Needed Help	
Did Themselves	

CARE SCHEDULE	TIME
Food & Drink Consumption	

CARE SCHEDULE	TIME
Bathroom	

MEDICATION / TREATMENT NOTES

SUCCESSFUL ACTIVITIES

OTHER NOTES / CONCERNS

DAILY REFLECTION

What Worked? Positives	What Didn't Work? Negatives

Date

MOOD	TIME(S)	NOTES
☐ Happy		
☐ Grumpy		
☐ Tired		
☐ Energetic		
☐ Frustrated		
☐ Confused		
☐ Calm		
☐ Quiet		
☐ Restless		
☐ Anger		
☐ Anxious		
☐ Fearful		
☐ Other		

CARE NEEDS	TIME
Needed Help	
Did Themselves	

CARE SCHEDULE	TIME
Food & Drink Consumption	

CARE SCHEDULE	TIME
Bathroom	

MEDICATION / TREATMENT NOTES

SUCCESSFUL ACTIVITIES

OTHER NOTES / CONCERNS

DAILY REFLECTION

What Worked? Positives	What Didn't Work? Negatives

Date

MOOD	TIME(S)	NOTES
☐ Happy		
☐ Grumpy		
☐ Tired		
☐ Energetic		
☐ Frustrated		
☐ Confused		
☐ Calm		
☐ Quiet		
☐ Restless		
☐ Anger		
☐ Anxious		
☐ Fearful		
☐ Other		

CARE NEEDS	TIME
Needed Help	
Did Themselves	

CARE SCHEDULE	TIME
Food & Drink Consumption	

CARE SCHEDULE	TIME
Bathroom	

MEDICATION / TREATMENT NOTES

SUCCESSFUL ACTIVITIES

OTHER NOTES / CONCERNS

DAILY REFLECTION

What Worked? Positives	What Didn't Work? Negatives

Date

MOOD	TIME(S)	NOTES
☐ Happy		
☐ Grumpy		
☐ Tired		
☐ Energetic		
☐ Frustrated		
☐ Confused		
☐ Calm		
☐ Quiet		
☐ Restless		
☐ Anger		
☐ Anxious		
☐ Fearful		
☐ Other		

CARE NEEDS	TIME
Needed Help	
Did Themselves	

CARE SCHEDULE	TIME
Food & Drink Consumption	

CARE SCHEDULE	TIME
Bathroom	

MEDICATION / TREATMENT NOTES

SUCCESSFUL ACTIVITIES

OTHER NOTES / CONCERNS

DAILY REFLECTION	
What Worked? Positives	What Didn't Work? Negatives

Date

MOOD	TIME(S)	NOTES
☐ Happy		
☐ Grumpy		
☐ Tired		
☐ Energetic		
☐ Frustrated		
☐ Confused		
☐ Calm		
☐ Quiet		
☐ Restless		
☐ Anger		
☐ Anxious		
☐ Fearful		
☐ Other		

CARE NEEDS	TIME
Needed Help	
Did Themselves	

CARE SCHEDULE	TIME
Food & Drink Consumption	

CARE SCHEDULE	TIME
Bathroom	

MEDICATION / TREATMENT NOTES

SUCCESSFUL ACTIVITIES

OTHER NOTES / CONCERNS

DAILY REFLECTION

What Worked? Positives	What Didn't Work? Negatives

Weekly Recap & Patterns

MAIN MOOD(S) / TIMES / PATTERNS

CARE NEEDS PATTERNS	CARE SCHEDULE PATTERNS
Needed Help	**Food & Drink Consumption**
Did Themselves	

CARE SCHEDULE PATTERNS	MEDICATION / TREATMENT NOTES
Bathroom	

SUCCESSFUL WEEKLY ACTIVITIES	OTHER NOTES / WEEKLY CONCERNS

WEEKLY REFLECTION	
What Worked? Positives	What Didn't Work? Negatives

Date

MOOD	TIME(S)	NOTES
☐ Happy		
☐ Grumpy		
☐ Tired		
☐ Energetic		
☐ Frustrated		
☐ Confused		
☐ Calm		
☐ Quiet		
☐ Restless		
☐ Anger		
☐ Anxious		
☐ Fearful		
☐ Other		

CARE NEEDS	TIME
Needed Help	
Did Themselves	

CARE SCHEDULE	TIME
Food & Drink Consumption	

CARE SCHEDULE	TIME
Bathroom	

MEDICATION / TREATMENT NOTES

SUCCESSFUL ACTIVITIES

OTHER NOTES / CONCERNS

DAILY REFLECTION

What Worked? Positives	What Didn't Work? Negatives

Date

MOOD	TIME(S)	NOTES
☐ Happy		
☐ Grumpy		
☐ Tired		
☐ Energetic		
☐ Frustrated		
☐ Confused		
☐ Calm		
☐ Quiet		
☐ Restless		
☐ Anger		
☐ Anxious		
☐ Fearful		
☐ Other		

CARE NEEDS	TIME
Needed Help	
Did Themselves	

CARE SCHEDULE	TIME
Food & Drink Consumption	

CARE SCHEDULE	TIME
Bathroom	

MEDICATION / TREATMENT NOTES

SUCCESSFUL ACTIVITIES

OTHER NOTES / CONCERNS

DAILY REFLECTION

What Worked? Positives	What Didn't Work? Negatives

Date

MOOD	TIME(S)	NOTES
☐ Happy		
☐ Grumpy		
☐ Tired		
☐ Energetic		
☐ Frustrated		
☐ Confused		
☐ Calm		
☐ Quiet		
☐ Restless		
☐ Anger		
☐ Anxious		
☐ Fearful		
☐ Other		

CARE NEEDS	TIME
Needed Help	
Did Themselves	

CARE SCHEDULE	TIME
Food & Drink Consumption	

CARE SCHEDULE	TIME
Bathroom	

MEDICATION / TREATMENT NOTES

SUCCESSFUL ACTIVITIES

OTHER NOTES / CONCERNS

DAILY REFLECTION

What Worked? Positives	What Didn't Work? Negatives

Date

MOOD	TIME(S)	NOTES
☐ Happy		
☐ Grumpy		
☐ Tired		
☐ Energetic		
☐ Frustrated		
☐ Confused		
☐ Calm		
☐ Quiet		
☐ Restless		
☐ Anger		
☐ Anxious		
☐ Fearful		
☐ Other		

CARE NEEDS	TIME
Needed Help	
Did Themselves	

CARE SCHEDULE	TIME
Food & Drink Consumption	

CARE SCHEDULE	TIME
Bathroom	

MEDICATION / TREATMENT NOTES

SUCCESSFUL ACTIVITIES

OTHER NOTES / CONCERNS

DAILY REFLECTION	
What Worked? Positives	What Didn't Work? Negatives

Date

MOOD	TIME(S)	NOTES
☐ Happy		
☐ Grumpy		
☐ Tired		
☐ Energetic		
☐ Frustrated		
☐ Confused		
☐ Calm		
☐ Quiet		
☐ Restless		
☐ Anger		
☐ Anxious		
☐ Fearful		
☐ Other		

CARE NEEDS	TIME
Needed Help	
Did Themselves	

CARE SCHEDULE	TIME
Food & Drink Consumption	

CARE SCHEDULE	TIME
Bathroom	

MEDICATION / TREATMENT NOTES

SUCCESSFUL ACTIVITIES

OTHER NOTES / CONCERNS

DAILY REFLECTION

What Worked? Positives	What Didn't Work? Negatives

Date

MOOD	TIME(S)	NOTES
☐ Happy		
☐ Grumpy		
☐ Tired		
☐ Energetic		
☐ Frustrated		
☐ Confused		
☐ Calm		
☐ Quiet		
☐ Restless		
☐ Anger		
☐ Anxious		
☐ Fearful		
☐ Other		

CARE NEEDS	TIME
Needed Help	
Did Themselves	

CARE SCHEDULE	TIME
Food & Drink Consumption	

CARE SCHEDULE	TIME
Bathroom	

MEDICATION / TREATMENT NOTES

SUCCESSFUL ACTIVITIES

OTHER NOTES / CONCERNS

DAILY REFLECTION

What Worked? Positives	What Didn't Work? Negatives

Date

MOOD	TIME(S)	NOTES
☐ Happy		
☐ Grumpy		
☐ Tired		
☐ Energetic		
☐ Frustrated		
☐ Confused		
☐ Calm		
☐ Quiet		
☐ Restless		
☐ Anger		
☐ Anxious		
☐ Fearful		
☐ Other		

CARE NEEDS	TIME
Needed Help	
Did Themselves	

CARE SCHEDULE	TIME
Food & Drink Consumption	

CARE SCHEDULE	TIME
Bathroom	

MEDICATION / TREATMENT NOTES

SUCCESSFUL ACTIVITIES

OTHER NOTES / CONCERNS

DAILY REFLECTION

What Worked? Positives	What Didn't Work? Negatives

Weekly Recap & Patterns

MAIN MOOD(S) / TIMES / PATTERNS

CARE NEEDS PATTERNS	CARE SCHEDULE PATTERNS
Needed Help	**Food & Drink Consumption**
Did Themselves	

CARE SCHEDULE PATTERNS	MEDICATION / TREATMENT NOTES
Bathroom	

SUCCESSFUL WEEKLY ACTIVITIES	OTHER NOTES / WEEKLY CONCERNS

WEEKLY REFLECTION

What Worked? Positives	What Didn't Work? Negatives

Made in the USA
Coppell, TX
02 March 2024

29674522R00083